I0094685

Piano, How Are You!

A Guide to Understand,
Evaluate & Maintain Your Piano

Published by

KKeelow Publishing

22 Auman Street

Devens, Massachusetts 01434

Library of Congress Control Number: 2015915712

ISBN: 978-0-9863337-0-5

Before performing any suggestions from this book, such as the
dismantling or testing of any piano, always consult the owner for
permission. No liability is assumed with respect to the use of the
information contained in this book.

Special thanks to: Lynn Y. Keel, Jamie Monat, Linda Varone, Claudia L. Wing, Adrian Leone, Jane Puffer, John Aberdeen and Kristine Rencs for your thoughts, assistance and encouragement.

Thanks to all of my clients who asked me so many questions about pianos, I was inspired to write this book!

And Best Wishes to my Mom,
Barbara C. Keel, Weaver Extraordinaire

And to my Dad,
Daniel Keel, Triple Rated Tuskegee Airman, living life to its fullest!

About This Book

You, Too, Can Assess a Piano!
Let this book act as your guide to select and maintain a piano that will bring you great enjoyment over the years.

Save Money before you contact a qualified technician.

Learn How to Test and Evaluate a piano.

Understand Methods Used by Technicians to keep a piano in optimum condition.

Find Out How to Locate an Expert in your area.

Learn to Recognize unusual sounds.

Know When to Contact a qualified tuner-technician.

View Photographs to identify different piano styles.

Protect Your Investment by understanding how to care for your instrument.

Enjoy the Stories In This Book about Keena Keel's unusual piano experiences.

Contents

Contents

Introduction

Why an individual likes a particular piano is subjective. This can vary from the type of sound one likes to hear, the feel of the piano, the color of the instrument, how it sounds in a particular room and more. It is important to find the piano that is right for you. There can be ten pianos in a room that are the same make and model and each of them may have a unique sound and touch.

The piano is a percussion instrument* that has been known to relieve stress when striking the keys. Due to its extensive range of notes from the low bass to the high treble, it is quite versatile. One can write or notate music for all the other instruments.

As a piano owner, it is important to maintain your investment. This book will educate you on what needs to be done. By following simple tests that are provided in the following chapters, you can learn to appreciate the sound and feel of a complex and magnificent instrument. You will also learn to know when it is time to contact a qualified technician to adjust a piano that does not sound or feel quite right.

Smithsonian Music, 2013

Have you had questions about your piano from time to time?

This book is designed to answer everyday questions that I have been asked repeatedly while servicing my clients. It includes telling stories of unusual encounters that I have had as a piano tuner-technician.

If you are looking to buy a piano, there are questions that you can ask to assist you in your purchase. Different piano styles are presented in the following chapters to assist you with understanding their levels of efficiency. They are the Spinet, Console, Studio, Full Upright and Grand pianos. Even when you have a tight budget, you may find after reviewing this book that you should focus in on one style that will serve your needs.

This book will explore your quest to find a suitable piano and maintain it appropriately. The Piano Technicians Guild* membership identifies experts in the field. I will refer to them as qualified technicians. I will also address why and how you can find an expert in your area.

* *Appendix*

1

First Inquiries

1. First Inquiries

You want to know more about your piano or you are shopping for a new piano. How exciting! What questions should you ask? First inquiries can save you time and money.

If you are not sure and want to know what style piano you have or should consider, read through the entire book first, and then revisit the chapters on piano styles, including modern players.

Does the owner have a warranty for this piano?

If this is a piano that is less than ten years old, does it still have a warranty? Is it transferrable? Was it purchased from a local dealer who will know the answer to this question?

Does it have a climate control system?

Climate control systems have a five year warranty. How old is this system? Is the warranty paperwork still available? When the owner does not have the paperwork, it should have been kept on file by the qualified technician who installed the system. It is standard procedure for the installer to register each system with the humidity control company, Piano Life Saver Systems. Having a climate control system is a benefit.

When was the piano last tuned?

Ask the current owner when the piano was last tuned. An in-tune piano is more pleasant to play, listen to, and may assist in a sale. It makes it easier to evaluate.

If the piano has not been tuned in the past year and you are considering whether or not to buy it, ask the owners if they would be willing to have it tuned before you come. Even when not in use, pianos have a tendency to go out of tune seasonally. You will need to hear the quality of the sound. If they refuse your request, ask for the name and telephone number of their piano tuner. This individual may be able to vouch for the piano's stability.

If their tuner does not remember the piano or if they do not have a piano tuner, you will have to decide whether or not you are willing to hire a qualified tuner* before you see the piano.

This is an added expense. But do you want to gamble? If the piano does not hold its tune, you will want to know this before making an offer.

Can you look inside the piano?

This book will provide you with a guide to assist you with peering inside to recognize older, newer and questionable parts. Ask the owners if they know how their piano opens and if they would be comfortable with you looking inside. If they are not sure how their piano opens, ask them if they would permit you to open the

*Appendix

piano with their assistance to view the inside when you arrive. Instructions on how to open piano styles will be presented in the following chapters, so you will be knowledgeable!

I would also suggest that you be wary of any piano that is listed for free. "Free" can be a deceptive term! I have had more than one client move a free piano to their home and business establishment and then ask me to assess it. Some of these new owners have paid piano movers hundreds of dollars to move them to only find out that it would cost thousands of dollars to restore them.

If you do not get permission to look inside the instrument, and the piano has not been tuned in a long while and will not be tuned for you, move on to another piano. This is an investment for you. Mistakes can be costly.

This book will provide you with a basic overview that will educate you to the point that you may want a qualified technician to view the instrument for you after you have seen it. After all, you want to make sure that it is technically sound. You will have heard how it sounds, know how it feels, seen the condition of some of its parts and have determined that you are definitely interested in pursuing this piano as a potential purchase. After reading through this book you will be educated on potential questions to ask a qualified technician!

During initial inquiries, involve the persons who will actually be playing the piano as they will know what is pleasing to them. They will need to experience how the piano feels as well as hear the quality of sound.

I am often asked, "What are some of the most interesting situations that you have come across while working on a piano?"

One such story that makes me smile is the visit from a woman who jingled. On this particular day I was prepping a piano for a performance on the top level of a store front. Suddenly, I was interrupted by a noise slowly coming up the stairs. A woman emerged. She jingled with each step that she took. She had little bells in her braided blonde hair. There were bells around her arms, attached to her clothing, around her legs and on her shoes!

When she reached the top of the stairs, the noise increased! It was now impossible for me to hear the strings vibrate in the piano.

So, I let her know that I could not hear while she jingled. She told me that she was participating in a sound healing workshop in this room in a few hours and needed to prepare the space for the guests. I could tell by her festive wear and her enthusiasm that the group was going to have a blast that night! I didn't want to burst her bubble, but I was running out of time.

The jingling woman assured me that she could be quiet. But it did not work. As she attempted to move in slow motion, I knew that I would have to tune the piano in-between her movements.

*Patience **is** a virtue!*

2

How Do I Sound?

2. How Do I Sound?

Now let's investigate sound and listen to a piano by applying simple tests.

Even Sounds

You will be listening for an even sound as you progressively play each key of the piano. Begin by playing one note at a time from the bass all the way up to the last treble note. Then play each note from the treble all the way down to the bass.

Bass   Tenor   Treble

Even if the piano is out of tune, do the notes sound like they are moving chromatically or consistently higher as you go up the scale and chromatically lower as you go down the scale? If so, they pass the first listening test.

(Pass) (Continue Testing)

Three finches sat on a perch in a cage. When I tuned the tenor notes, one bird would sing. When I tuned the treble notes, another bird would sing. And when I tuned the bass, the third finch would sing. It was soothing. They knew their pitch.

Out of Tune Sections

Is there a dramatic break with a complete section of notes, and the bass section sounds like it suddenly dropped two octaves from the tenor and treble sections? Or, vice versa? If this extreme change exists, then there is most probably a problem with the bridges of the piano coming apart at the soundboard or they may contain large cracks. The wooden bridges hold the strings.

The bridge in the photo only contains some small cracks. This is not major.

Bridge separation and large cracks could result in a costly repair.
(Fail) (Move On to Another Piano)
or ***(Hire a Technician)***

Ringing Notes

Do any of the bass, tenor or treble notes continue to sound after you have released a key? If so, the dampers may be worn and in need of replacement.

Strings

Dampers

Hammers

Note that the top section of treble strings do not have any dampers. These strings are only inches long in this area of the piano and have a short sound.

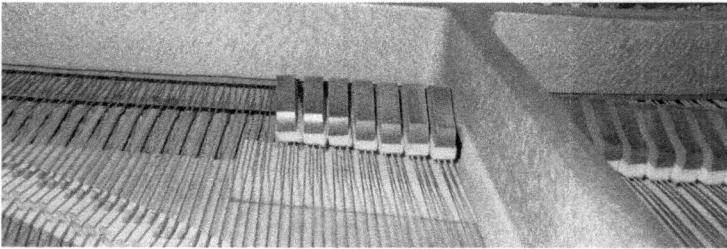

If the notes with dampers on top of the strings do not ring after release of the key, the piano passes the "no ringing" test. **(Pass)**

The cost of damper replacements, should they be necessary, is a question for a qualified technician. If replacement costs fall within your budget, then the piano "passes with replacement". **(Pass)**

I had a client who called to tell me that her piano kept ringing all of the time. When I opened the piano to look at the condition of the dampers, I discovered that all of the felt on the dampers was missing. She asked her husband to guess what I had found. He knew right away ... "Mice," he said. "This is an old farmhouse."

Unrecognizable Sounds

If the piano sounds extremely out of tune or has some wild sounding notes, then it is possible that it has loose tuning pins that need to be replaced. This would require verification by a qualified technician.

(Questionable)

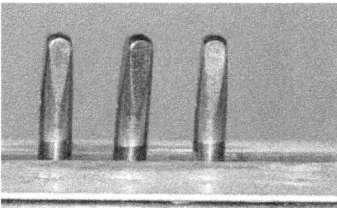

Nickel Tuning Pins

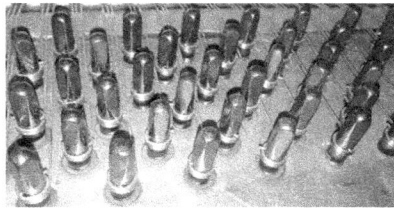

Blued Tuning Pins

The strings are attached to tuning pins. They are adjusted to tune more than two hundred strings. There are two basic colors that you may see: nickel or blue.

21

Not sure if the piano is extremely out of tune? Ask the individual who will be playing the instrument to play a song. Can you recognize the tune? Can anyone recognize the tune?

(Questionable Until Tuned)

Don't mind paying to replace parts?

(Pass)

You do mind paying to replace worn parts.

(Fail) (Move On to Another Piano)

You do not like the sound of this out-of-tune piano.

(Fail) (Move on to Another Piano)

Overall Observations

The piano you have been testing has a pleasant sound. It does not appear to have any significant sound problems. You do not mind addressing minor concerns, as repairs are within your budget.

(Pass)

(Proceed to the Following Chapter)

3

Am I Quiet?

3. Am I Quiet?

A quiet piano with no shake, rattle or buzz is a healthy piano.

A parrot was sitting on a perch next to the piano that I was about to tune. The owner let me know that the parrot liked opera and then she left me to work. I struck several notes in the middle of the piano while tuning. Suddenly, a noise rattled in the piano. The parrot squawked "Oh, no!" And I turned my head to tell the parrot that I would certainly fix the problem, but not at that moment.

When I struck a key in the higher treble the parrot sang a beautiful operatic note. So I acknowledged that this must be its favorite opera range. Then I continued my task.

As my tuning led me back to the rattle in the middle of the piano the bird yelled out "Well, help!"

With my eyes and mouth wide open I told the parrot "I'll take care of it right away!" I did not want to offend its musical sensibilities. I wondered what it would have told its owner?

Do I Rattle?

Play each note on the piano loudly, moving from the bass end to the treble end. Do you hear any rattling?

Does it only happen when you play certain notes? It is possible that an object could be touching the soundboard or that there is an object sitting on the back of the keys like a pen or pencil.

The soundboard can be checked in a vertical or upright piano by looking behind the instrument. Make sure you look to the bottom as well.

If you hear a rattle in a grand piano when you play, you will have to visually look at the soundboard to see if there is an object resting on top of it. If the rattle sounds like it is closer to the keys while you play, then it could simply be a pencil that dropped in and is moving around.

Opening piano cases will be addressed in the chapters on piano styles. Pencils, paper clips, toys and other surprises that fall inside the piano can only be removed when the case is open.

Cannot locate the rattle.

(Questionable Until Case Removed & Checked)

25

If you find an object touching the backside of an upright soundboard, remove it. A grand piano is less accessible and may require a technician.

Did the rattle stop? Yes.

(Pass)

If the rattle cannot be located it will have to be checked by a technician.

You will have to decide whether to call a technician or move on to another piano.

(Questionable, Your Decision)

A baby grand piano had a loud buzzing noise that was irritating my client. I thought that it may be coming from the soundboard, but I did not see anything sitting on top of it to make it vibrate. Then suddenly I saw one tiny link from a silver chain. Once I removed it, the sound disappeared. Although the buzz was loud, the cause was minor.

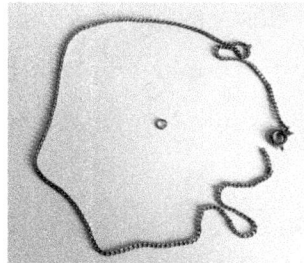

Do I Have a Buzz?

Do you hear a distinct buzzing when you play one note? This could be caused by a sympathetic vibration coming from another object in the room. When you strike the note, it vibrates at the same frequency of sound as the object. The buzz could come from a wall hanging, a light fixture, a loose screw, a snare drum head or more.

One day I arrived at the home of a schoolmaster to tune an old full upright piano. He lived in a private academy. When I struck the first note, I heard a rattle. It sounded like it was coming from the back of the piano. When I pulled the piano away from the wall, I found two castanets resting along the back of the soundboard. When you played the piano, they would play their percussive sound along with the piano like you would find in a drum set!

No one knew how these items got there. I'm pretty sure that they fell off the top of the piano one day. Since it was located in and old prestigious school, it probably had numerous visitors throughout

its time. The irony of the situation was that the owners thought the piano was supposed to sound that way!

More Than One Buzz?

Do you hear a distinct buzzing when you play more than one note? This could indicate that one or more objects are touching the soundboard. It could also indicate that a crack has developed in the soundboard or elsewhere in the piano and is vibrating.

Diagonal ribs hold the back of the soundboard. Objects that have fallen behind an upright piano and into its bottom half can create noise.

In a grand piano the top of the soundboard is under the strings. The diagonal ribs would be underneath the soundboard.

If a glue joint comes undone between the ribs and the back of the soundboard, the piano may vibrate.

If you are unable to discover where the noise is coming from right away, you will have to decide whether to call for technical assistance or move forward with your inspection process. A qualified technician would need to be contacted to look at the extent of this problem and provide you with a repair estimate.

Cannot locate the buzzing?
(Questionable Until Checked by a Technician)

Buzz & Rattle Free!

Great. Time to move to the next chapter to observe your personal preferences.
(Pass)

Don't want additional expenses? Time to move on to another piano.
(Fail)

I received a call for help one day from one of my clients. She mentioned that her child was complaining about a noise in the piano. Whenever her child played one particular note in the middle of the grand piano she would hear a buzzing noise.

Well, sure enough it was easy to identify which note was creating the noise. But where was the noise coming from in the room? It was a sympathetic vibration.

Each time I would strike the note, I would have my client hold onto a different object in the room to see if the hum would stop. After our tenth attempt, we were getting frustrated. It was terribly annoying! In a last ditch effort I had my client hold the metronome that was now sitting on a bookcase.

Bingo! No more noise.

4

Personal Preferences

4. Personal Preferences

You are comfortable and accepting of the attributes of the piano based on the previous tests. Now it is time to observe your personal preferences.

Feel

When the pianist who will be playing the piano sits down at the piano bench and begins to play, how does the piano feel to them?

*   Do the keys feel loose, tight or just right?
*   Do they respond evenly or do some keys stick?

If it is difficult to push down on the the keys, the friction will need to be inspected by a technician who can then provide you with a repair estimate. It could be a simple repair, but only a qualified technician can give you an estimate.

You like the feel of the piano?
(Pass)

> *A small, grey, short-haired cat with one glassy eye approached the piano as I sat down on the piano bench. The owners noticed that I was observing her and said to me, "The cat is useless. It has a diseased eye."*

The couple left me alone and the animal sat attentively, staring at the piano as I prepared to work on the instrument.

I worked for a piano dealer in New Hampshire at the time and the piano had only arrived an hour earlier. In this remote White Mountain location, I imagined that the cat had few visitors and this new instrument peaked the interest of Mademoiselle cat. Suddenly, she jumped up on the piano bench, sat beside me and began to play notes one at a time with her paw.

Do you think she was testing the touch? :-)

Tone

* Does the sound come back in an even tone? Nice.
* Are some notes brighter or louder than others? If they are, the hammers may need adjustments called voicing. This could include re-shaping worn parts or needling loud hammers to soften their sound.

You like the tone of the piano?

(Pass)

Hammers in Great Shape

*Worn Hammers Create
Uneven Sound*

You do not mind spending a little more to re-furbish worn parts.
(Pass)

Pedal Play

While the pianist is playing, the pedals should be depressed to
make sure that they are working.

Soft Pedal　　　　*Damper Pedal*

The pedal on the right lifts the dampers away
from the strings so the notes will not be muffled
when played.

The left pedal is the soft pedal designed to soften the sounds while notes are being played.

In an *Upright*, the hammers will move closer to the strings or be softened by a felt flag that drops down between the hammers and the strings.

In a *Grand* piano the left pedal, known as the una corda, or soft pedal, will shift the entire keyboard to the right. It allows notes that have 2 strings to shift over to one string and notes that have 3 strings to play 2 of the 3 strings to soften the sound.

The middle pedal is the one pedal that varies in piano styles. In an *Upright Piano* the middle pedal may push the bass hammer section closer to the strings to give them a softer sound. The pedal could also serve as a place holder with absolutely no function at all.

In a *Grand Piano* the middle pedal is called the sostenuto or sustain pedal. It lifts a rail that allows the pianist to hold down a chord and then allows the pianist to play single notes on top of the chord as the chord sustains its tone. There are some grand pianos that have three pedals but the middle pedal is not designed to work.

Some pianos only have two pedals. If this is the case, the soft pedal is still on the left and the damper pedal is always on the right.

In some of the newer upright pianos the three pedals will act in the same way they do in a grand piano. The middle pedal is designed to be a sostenuto or sustain pedal.

Without the eye of a qualified technician you may not know whether or not the middle pedal, if there is one, should function or if it is broken.

So the two most important pedals for your initial testing are the right pedal for damping and the left pedal if you have a need to soften the piano while playing.

Pedals that you require for playing are working. Great!
(Pass)

The grand pedal box, which is the encasement that holds the pedals in place, is also referred to as the lyre or trapwork.* Some of the boxes are actually shaped like the Greek stringed instrument called the Lyre. This is a U-shaped harp.

* *Steinway Parts Catalogue*

Each of the rods in this pedal mechanism must be mounted correctly for the piano to function as it is designed. Some lyres are connected to the piano by a lock & key design. Others are screwed in.

Please remember to contact a piano technician for the name of a qualified piano mover!

I have noticed that when individuals do not know who to call to move their pianos and have no references, they tend to call the mover with the name that starts with the first letter of the alphabet. I have been called on more than several occasions to refer a competent piano mover to correct a problem with a grand and upright piano that would not play after an unknown "AAA" moving company broke off a pedal, dropped the piano or attempted to re-assemble the piano incorrectly.

The two most common problems that I have encountered with movers who have no piano knowledge are their incorrect re-mounting of grand piano legs and their confusion with how to reassemble the pedals.

The client discovers immediately that the piano keeps ringing, the treble keys do not work, or the pedals do not function properly. I would recommend keeping your expenses down by hiring an experienced piano mover who also has insurance.

5

Am I the Piano for You ?

5. Am I the Piano For You?

Observe Where I Am Located

The ideal humidity for piano stability is approximately 40 to 50 percent with a temperature of approximately 70 degrees Fahrenheit or 21.1 degrees Celsius. *

Make note of the following:

- Is the piano close to radiator heat? This is not a plus.
  (Questionable Until Checked by a Technician)

- Is the piano in a room where the temperature and humidity can change drastically with the seasons? These conditions may foster mold or other problems. This is not a plus.
  (Questionable Until Checked by a Technician)

- Is the instrument near or on the ocean or another body of water? Parts will probably rust and require routine replacement. If the piano is moved to a dry location, it will probably crack.
  (Questionable Until Checked by a Technician)

- Is it in the same room with a wood burning stove and has cracks? This is not a plus.
  (Questionable Until Checked by a Technician)

* *PianoLifeSaver.com*

- Is it near an outside door that is frequently opened and closed? It will need to be tuned at least seasonally.
  (Questionable Until Checked by a Technician)

- Is the room humid, dry or comfortable ?
  Humid is not good and too dry is not good. Climatically controlled is just right. A climate control system will help maintain stability.
  (Pass)

Final Questions

The final step is a series of questions for you. Anything that does not pass will be noted as a question that needs to be answered to your satisfaction or needs an estimated repair cost from a qualified piano technician.

- Do all of the notes play (usually 88)? Yes ***(Pass)***
- Are any of the keys sticking or sluggish? No ***(Pass)***
- Have you noted any other problems? No ***(Pass)***

You have listened to the instrument, felt its response, enjoy its sound, and initially accepted the piano you are viewing. Now stand back and look to see if you want this particular instrument in your home, school, church, theatre, concert venue or business establishment.

- Can you live with the way the case looks? Yes *(Pass)*
- Do you like the color? Yes *(Pass)*
- Do you accept any nicks and scratches? Yes *(Pass)*
- Do you mind if the keytops are cracked? No. *(Pass)*

If you like this piano and do not mind paying extra in the event that you would want to make some improvements, it passes and is a candidate for further evaluation. It is time to open up the piano and look inside before calling a qualified technician.

You are looking at either a grand, full or studio upright, console or spinet piano. The condition of the parts may aid you in deciding whether or not to keep the instrument you have, get it refurbished, sell it, or buy the piano you are presently investigating.

Learn to communicate with a qualified technician. This may include forwarding a photo by email.

6

View the Condition of My Parts

6. View the Condition of My Parts

If you have decided to look at the parts inside the piano of your choice, the following chapters will cover more specific information on the piano style you have chosen. Viewing the inside of a piano will give you some idea of the age and condition of the instrument.

Each of these chapters describes how to peer inside and recognize parts that appear to be in good condition as well as parts that appear to be worn. When a qualified technician speaks with you about the inside of the piano it should not be a totally foreign subject to you.

Tools You May Need to Open Me

The exceptionally beautiful casework on a given piano does not mean that it will be a wonderful piano to play. If you were given permission to check the inside of a vertical or upright piano you may need the following tools to open it. Pianos have many different cabinet styles. Be prepared. If you are not handy, you will need to ask if the owner can do this for you, or contact a qualified piano technician. We all have different aptitudes.

If you are viewing a *Grand Piano*, bring with you:

- A tape measure
- A flashlight
- A camera, if the owner will let you take photo notes

In a grand piano you can see the condition of many significant parts by looking through the top of the piano with the music desk removed. You will need a tape measure to measure the length of the piano. A flashlight will be required if the room is dark. And a camera will help you remember what you saw.

How to remove the music desk and safely lift up the top will be discussed in the chapter on Grand Styles.

If you are viewing an *Upright Piano* bring with you:

- A straight edge screwdriver
- A phillips head screwdriver
- A flashlight
- A tape measure to measure the height of the piano
- A camera, if the owner will let you take photo notes

Let's explore what type of piano you are investigating, how to open it up, and what to look for to note if this is a potential prize.

You May Need Permission

Always ask the owner for permission and assistance
before opening the instrument.

If it is not clear to you how to open the instrument, please ask the
owner if they will do it for you. If the owner does not know how
the piano opens, wait until a technician is with you and the owner.

DO NOT OPEN
WITHOUT OWNER'S PERMISSION

7

Am I a Spinet Piano?

7. Am I a Spinet Piano?

The Spinet Piano
36"-40" from floor to closed top

The Spinet, named after the initiating inventor Giovanni Spinetti
of Venice, began its evolution in 1503 as a small harpsichord-
like, boxed instrument. By the end of the 16th Century, a
prototype of the Spinet Style was developed. Changes continued
to be made over time until remnants of the harpsichord style
were left behind and it became a small piano. *

My True Identity

The Spinet Piano can be identified as the shortest of the upright
or vertical styles. The keyboard width is the same as any other
regular vertical piano with 88 keys.

* *Pianos And Their Makers, 1972*

Hammers

Keys

Due to the spinet's short height, the action, which can also be referred to as the moving parts of the piano, is located above and below the keys. This is referred to as a drop action. The hammers rest slightly above the backs of the keys. When a key is struck, the action begins.

If you want to observe the rest of the action, the bottom case panel must be opened. Also note that the backs of the keys are usually connected to wires or long wooden stickers, with or without a rail, that can be seen looking down towards the bottom of the piano. This is how they interact with the piano action below. The action is the mechanism that allows the piano to play as a unit, like the engine of an automobile.

Regardless of what they name the piano, it can only be identified by its action style. The hammers are above the keys, and the remaining piano action extends below the keys in all Spinet Pianos, as in the photo below.

Open My Top

In order to view the insides of the piano you must first lift open the top of the piano. It may lift up from the music desk, as in the full front desk style seen in the first photo of this chapter on page 48. A prop is being used to hold the top open in this photo. However, you will need to have someone hold it open for you. This is a common style.

Another style is designed to open by lifting the top up and back toward the wall as seen below.

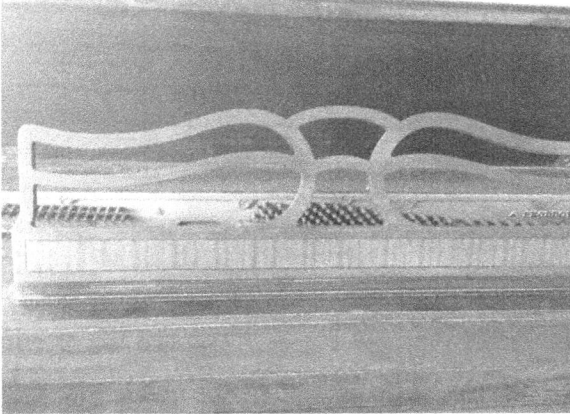

Music Desk

As you have opened up the top, you can now peer down with a flashlight if necessary and see if the front section is hooked on pegs, held by hinge pins or screwed in on each side.

Once the front is released it may then slide forward toward you or you might have to lift it straight up. Please ask the owner. If you are the owner, you will have to ask your technician.

51

A less common Spinet may have a top that lifts up from right to left. If this is the case, ask someone to hold it up while you take a look inside. It would be easier to manage and faster. In any case, never force a piece to open.

Release My Bottom

To open the bottom of the piano, look for a latch to be pushed up to release the panel. This is the most common. Push up the latch and pull the panel towards you at a 45 degree angle with two hands. Then lift it up and out slowly.

Pushing up on this latch allows you to open the bottom panel

Some Spinets have hinge pins located at each side of the bottom panel. Pull out the hinge pins and open up the panel. Be careful when you lift the panel. It may be heavy and it may be slippery.

I like to pull the bottom panel forward at a 45 degree angle and brace it against one knee. Do not do this alone. The panel may need to slide out from the sides, as the legs may be in the way.

It may also need to be lifted up and away from the pedals. Some casework is pretty fancy. If it is too fancy, you may not be able to look into the bottom half of the piano without the aid of a technician. If this is the case, concentrate on what you can see and hear.

What do you see inside?

Jot down what you see, so that you may question a technician if you decide to pursue this investment. Dark, worn and cracked parts may require repair or replacement. How much would this cost?

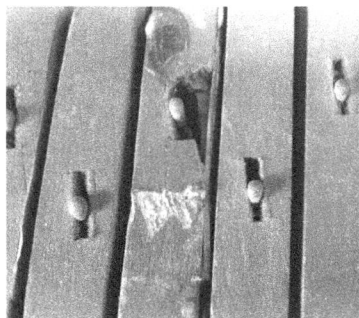

Take photos of the instrument to act as a reminder to you. What parts of the piano do you want to remember? Do you want to compare these photos to another piano that you are considering?

Strings

Dampers

Hammers

Action Rail

Backs of Keys

- *Are the hammer felts rather white looking?*
  These may be on the newer side. That would be a plus.

- *Do the hammers look worn and have deep grooves in them?*
  If so, you will need an estimate for refurbishing them or
  replacing them.

- *Are the strings rusty?* Parts in this condition are
  questionable. How long will they last?

- *When you look below do you see any cracks?*
  Finding no cracks is in your best interest. Cracks are
  questionable.

- *Do the parts look like new?* This is a bonus!

Take a photograph. It is a golden depiction.

Put Me Back Together

When the panel is put back into its original position, it should be aligned to the slots in the bottom of the casework. The slot will be either a groove or a groove with pegs to be aligned. Place the panel at a 45 degree angle and then push it back into the latch. Pull on it lightly to make sure that it is securely in place. Whatever style cabinet you take apart, please make sure that you put all of the pieces back in place.

Are My Parts Obsolete?

The Spinet Piano is being phased out of production. Some older Spinets were made with parts that can no longer be purchased from supply houses. This information can only be obtained by a piano technician.

My Level of Efficiency

The Spinet is the least responsive of all pianos. It takes a little more time for the mechanism to move the hammers to the strings so your fingers cannot play notes as quickly as they can on a taller vertical piano or a grand piano. This style may contain rubber or plastic pieces that are a part of the lifting mechanism. When they are old and worn they may crumble, crack, or fall off and become unadjustable. If the action sounds a bit noisy, this may be one of the contributing factors.

There are well-made Spinets that do have a pleasant sound. This is up to you to determine. What one likes in a piano is subjective.

The strings in a Spinet are the shortest piano strings in the vertical piano series due to its limited height. When parts become obsolete or begin to malfunction or break, this would be the time to consider an upgraded piano style.

Is My Spinet Style the Best Fit for You?

Anyone who likes the sound and feel of this piano would benefit by owning or purchasing it. The notes do not come back as fast as they do in a taller piano so it is possible that at some point the pianist may outgrow this style.

This is a piano style that many of us had in our homes during our childhoods and for some of us, they contain sentimental value.

Please note that this should be the least expensive piano style to purchase.

If you enjoy the sound and touch of this piano, it would be time to contact a Registered Piano Tuner Technician who is a member of the Piano Technician's Guild.* The technician will let you know whether or not the instrument is technically sound.

* *Appendix*

This would include testing the tuning pins to see if their torque is strong enough to hold a standard tuning.

In addition to finding candy, toys, pencils, pens, coins, paperclips, batteries, papers, elastic bands, books, jewelry, hair pins, seeds, nuts, castanets and a drum stick that have fallen or been placed in pianos, the most baffling item that I have found is a bagel with dried-up cream cheese.

These objects, which impede the piano's ability to function at its most efficient level, point to adventures that only the piano can tell.

My most rewarding piano tuning was for a young man in Massachusetts who was a paraplegic. He waited attentively by the piano until I finished. His eyes then lit up as he rolled his wheel chair toward the upright piano. When he began to play with all of his strength, I was mesmerized with delight. "No charge for this one, my friend," I said as I walked to the door to let myself out.

8

Am I a Console Piano?

8. Am I a Console Piano?

The Console Piano
40" - 46" from floor to closed top.*

The Upright or Vertical Piano was built in the late 1700's by Johann Schmidt of Austria. In 1826 Robert Worum of London developed a playing action that successfully inspired the designs that are used in modern pianos today.**

Open Me

The Console Piano can be as short as the tallest 40" Spinet Piano or slightly taller. When the panel that rests on top of the keys is lifted up, the keys are visible. This is called the fallboard.

---

* Ancott Associates Music Product Directory: Discontinued Keyboard Edition, Volume 8.
** Pianos and their Makers, 1972

The Fallboard covers the keys

Lift Up My Top

In order to view the insides of the piano you must first lift open the top of the piano case. It will usually be indicated by an open slit located below the ledge on top. It will lift back toward the wall.

If the piano is located too close to the wall, move it forward or have someone hold the top open for you. The opening in the photo below is the most common style.

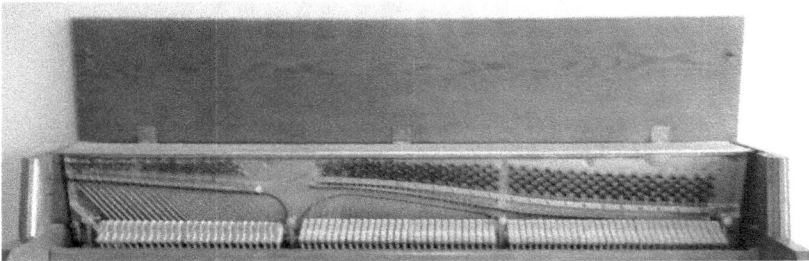

Pianos that have a long hinge on the left side top of the piano will lift up at an angle from the right side. You will need to have someone hold the top up while you look inside.

I Am Streamlined

When the front panel that holds the music desk is taken off, it exposes the piano action. This is the moving mechanism of the piano.

Piano Action

The keyboard width is the same as any other regular vertical piano. The string length or height, however, determines where the action will sit so the hammers will strike the strings as designed. As you can see, the piano mechanism is above the keytops rather than below, as it is in the Spinet Piano.

The Console is the shortest of the "above the key" piano actions. It is streamlined or more compact than a taller upright to make it move as efficiently as possible to accommodate the string length. As with the Spinet, regardless of what they name the piano, it can only be identified by its action style.

There are some pianos that are tricky to open. Fortunately, these are the least common styles.

After lifting up the top of the piano, the top front panel can be removed by looking inside from the top to see how it is fastened.

- You may need to lift up latches located on each side.
- You may need to lift it off hooks.
- It may just be resting on pegs or
- It will need to be unscrewed with a straight edge or phillips head screwdriver.

A flashlight would be prudent in instances where you need more light to see how the front is attached. The front panel may lift straight up or come out at an angle.

This style piano opens by lifting up a latch inside the front panel on each side. Sometimes you will just see screws that you will have to remove.

Never force a part to open.

Release My Bottom

Open the bottom of the piano. Look for one latch in the center of the panel or two latches, one on either side to push up and release at the same time. Pull the panel towards you. Be careful as the panel may be heavy. Do this with the owner.

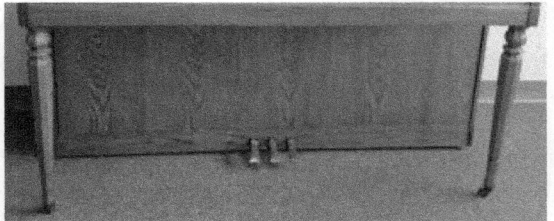

What Do You See Inside?

With both the top and bottom now open, what are the conditions of the parts that you see? Do they look worn, rusty, clean or new?

Is the wood dark like the worn and dirty parts below?

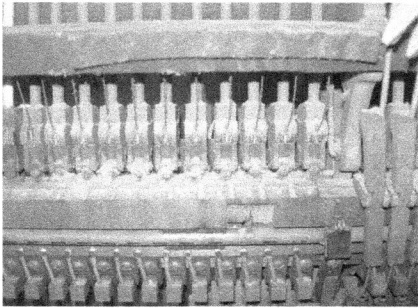

Do you notice any cracks in the soundboard? It is located under the strings. If there are cracks, are they wide or thin?

The Soundboard is behind the strings and the cast iron plate

If you are unable to see the condition of the parts because they are too dirty, ask if the owner(s) will hire a technician to clean the inside of the instrument. You would like to clearly view your potential investment. Parts that are not only dirty but dark as well, indicate that they are old and brittle. It may be difficult to predict how long they will last before they begin to break. Replacement costs are questions for qualified technicians.

Are the tuning pins and strings rusty? If so, they may break, produce a tinny sound or need to be replaced.

The hammers, dampers and strings to the left appear to be in great shape. They are light in color and the strings do not contain any rust.

Pianos that have parts that look like they are on the newer side are an investment possibility. The whole piano is not exempt from the technical scrutiny of a piano technician, however.

Jot Down What You See

Writing down what you observe will help you to remember questions that you may want to ask a technician if you decide to pursue this instrument. Dark, worn and cracked parts may require repair or replacement. These costs can be estimated by a qualified technician. Will the owner allow you to take photos?

Close Me Carefully

When the bottom panel is put back it should be aligned to the slots in the bottom. They may be peg holes or just a groove that is the length of the bottom panel. The top panel should be carefully placed back in its original position as well.

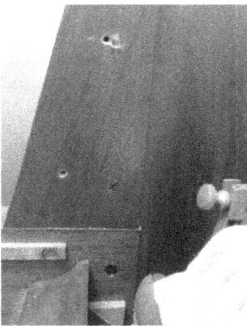

Please note that when you are finished and are about to put any screw back into the top panel, back the screw counter-clockwise first. This should allow you to feel it go into its old position before screwing it forward. This will prevent stripping the screw hole as seen in this photo.

My Level of Efficiency

When a key is played on a Console Piano, it can move slightly faster to the strings than the shorter Spinet Piano. With the action located above the keys, the hammers do not have to be lifted from below. This is a more efficient movement.

The strings are longer, in most cases, in a Console than they are in a Spinet. Usually the longer the piano string, the cleaner the sound. However, some Consoles as well as Spinets do not have a scale that was well designed and are inharmonious. This is apparent when played. The sound is not clean, but muddy. And it may be impossible for the piano tuner to make it sound cleaner. A piano with a well designed piano scale that produces a clean sound and responsive touch will be a gem of a piano.

The Piano Action Mechanism

Is My Console Style Right For You?

Anyone who likes the sound and feel of the Console piano they are playing would benefit by purchasing it; and anyone who does not need to play notes extremely fast would benefit.

If you are satisfied with what you see when you look inside, then it would be time to call a registered technician who is a member of the Piano Technicians Guild.*

Some members of my Piano Technicians Guild Chapter used to talk about a man who posed as an expert Piano Tuner-Technician. Whenever he encountered a problem with a piano he would use scotch tape to piece parts together. For example, "Oh, a broken hammer. Do you have any scotch tape?'

I said, "Really? Are you joking?"

Well, one day I received a call from someone I had never met. There was a problem with the piano. "Could I come over as soon as possible?" It was now my turn to follow this man's work. When

I saw the scotch tape repair, all I could do was laugh. He was famous! But now, the client had to pay again for the same repair, but this time with legitimate replacement parts.

---

* Appendix

I love the sound of the Vibrating String

9

Am I a Studio
or Full Upright Piano?

9. Am I a Studio or Full Upright Piano?

Studio Piano
Height ranges are 43"-47" high from floor to top of piano

Improvements were developed in the Upright Piano in 1826.
Thus began its popularity in Europe from London to Paris to
*Germany and in the late 1800s in America.**

Full Upright Piano
*48"-57.3"** high*

* Pianos and their Makers 1972
* *Bluthner Model S 57.3" tall

Studio and Full Upright Pianos are in the tallest upright piano category. The keyboard width with 88 keys is commonly the same as any other regular vertical piano. The action stack is located above the keys.

Full Uprights, also called Professional Uprights, have the tallest action stacks. This mechanism is designed to strike long strings. In theory, the longer the string the cleaner the sound. The full upright design also creates an efficient touch. You, however, will have to be the judge of its feel and sound as each piano is different. Some individuals enjoy a warm sound. Some individuals want to hear a bright sounding instrument. Taste varies.

Accessibility to My Top & Front

As one must do with a Console Piano, in order to view the insides of the piano you must first lift open the top of the piano case. It will usually be indicated by an open slit located below the ledge on top. It will lift back toward the wall. If the piano is located too close to the wall, move it forward or have someone hold the top open for you. This is a common style.

After lifting up the top of the piano case, the top front panel can be removed. Ask the owner to assist you. Look inside to see how it is attached. If there are latches located on each side, they will need to be moved away from the pegs that they are covering. It is possible that the panel may be screwed in on each side. You will have to use the appropriate screwdriver to release the panel.

The front panel could also be resting on pegs, or hooked over pegs. A flashlight would be prudent in some instances. The front panel may lift straight up or come out at an angle. If the front panel is heavy, please ask for assistance. Slowly move the panel up and toward you and the owner.

Two Panels Hinged Together

It is possible that the front panel may be connected to the cover over the keys, which is also called the fallboard. Be careful and move slowly. It may not be one piece but two case pieces that

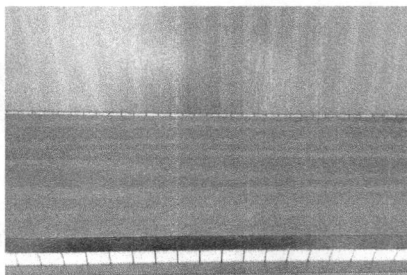

are attached to each other by a long hinge. This hinge will most probably be located several inches above the back of the keys.

I have seen this style present in some Samick pianos. As you begin to pull the front panel toward you and the casework above the keys begins to move with the top, then you know that they are attached to each other. If this is the case, please contact a technician. It is extremely important to be careful not to damage the instrument.

In any instance that it is not clear how to remove the front panel, please contact a piano technician. These panels can be slippery and heavy. Meanwhile, you can peer down through the top of the piano with a flashlight. In this way you can see whether the parts look worn.

Are My Pedals Working?

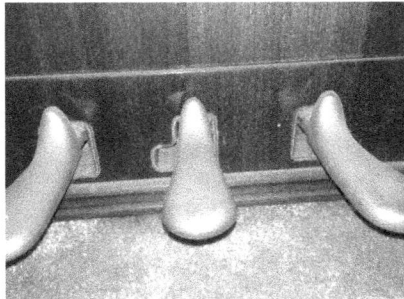

Left Pedal is the Soft Pedal

Right Pedal is the Damper Pedal

*Middle is the Soft Pedal with Locking Mechanism**

*Not all pedals are equipped with a locking mechanism to keep the soft pedal engaged

With the top and front revealed, you can watch the parts of the action that move when you push down on each pedal. The pedal on the right is the damper pedal, the most commonly played.

The middle and left pedals usually act as soft pedals. When working, they will either soften the sound as the hammers are pushed closer to the strings, or pull a felt flag

Flag Style

down in front of the hammers to soften the sound.

In some modern pianos, however, the middle pedal will act like the sostenuto pedal in a grand piano. When you play a chord, then put your foot on the sostenuto pedal, the chord will continue to ring. Then you can play single notes on top of that chord while you keep your foot on the pedal.

You may notice that some pianos only have two pedals. They are the soft pedal and the damper pedal.

Open My Bottom

Look for one latch in the center of the panel or two latches on either side to release at the same time. Push up on the

latches with your thumbs. Pull the top of the panel towards you.

It could also have a style with a
piece of wood located on the right
and left side of the bottom panel.
They can be turned out to release
the panel and turned in to brace
the panel.

Fancy case work may inhibit your moving the panel. The lyre may
be sitting on top of the pedals. This should only be removed by a
technician.

In all circumstances, be careful as the panel may be heavy. Do
this with the owner.

Single Latch Style

Harp

Soundboard

Wooden Bridges support the strings   *Bridge Pins guide the strings*

The harp of the piano in the photo on the previous page resembles the stringed harp instrument. The wooden panel behind the strings is called the soundboard.

What do you see inside?

Look at the condition of the tuning pins, strings, dampers, hammers, wooden parts, keytops and pedals. The initial tests that brought you to this piano indicated that the soundboard and bridges were acceptable.

Tuning Pins

Strings

Dampers

Hammers

- Do the tuning pins and strings look rusty? No. Great.
- Do the dampers look dark and worn? No. Great.
- Are the hammers white looking and smooth? Yes. Great.
- Do the wooden parts look old and worn? Refurbishing is an additional expense.

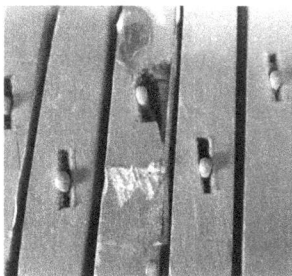 

Worn parts

- Are the keytops in good condition or are they chipped and cracked? They are acceptable for playing. Good.
- Are the pedals functioning properly? Yes. Good.
- As you look below do you notice any cracks? If so, are they thin cracks or wide gaps? Take a photo if this is a concern to you. Remember to address this issue with a technician.

Whether you are the owner or buyer, jot down any questions that you need to have addressed. This is an investment. It may be helpful to obtain an estimate for any potential repair or replacement work. If it is too dirty to see the condition of the parts, ask the owner if s(he) would hire a technician to clean the inside of the piano. If possible, take photos to keep as reminders of what you have observed.

I had been called by a client who said that whenever she pushed down on one key, ten keys went down at the same time. When I arrived and tried the piano, sure enough, multiple keys moved as I pushed down on one key. "Quite strange," I thought. So I proceeded to open up the upright piano to take out the keys. Suddenly, I spotted the hidden candle wax that had dripped between the keys. My client must have had a meditative piano session and then blew out the candles on the piano. Whoever wiped off the wax from the top of the keys, didn't notice the wax that had dripped down the sides, binding them together. Mystery solved.

I Need Closure

When the bottom panel of the piano is put back, it should be aligned to the slots in the bottom, whether they are peg holes or just a groove. The top panel should be put back in its slots as well.

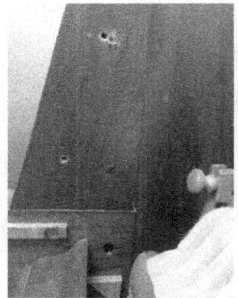

Please note that when you are finished and are about to put the screws back into the top panel, back each screw in first by twisting it counter-clockwise. This should allow you to feel it go into its old position before screwing it clockwise. This will prevent stripping the screw hole or making a new hole.

My Level of Efficiency

When the keys are played, the hammers move straight across to strike the strings.

The dampers rest against the strings to prevent them from ringing until a specific piano key is played. When the key is struck, the hammer moves toward the string as the damper moves back from the string to allow it to sing or play.

The Studio/Full Upright piano styles are designed to create the most efficient key movement for vertical pianos of this size. This style also allows the longest string length for upright pianos. A piano with a clean sound and amicable touch will be a gem of a piano. The Studio Upright has become a very popular style to buy.

Is My Style Best for You?

Anyone who likes the sound and feel of this piano would benefit by purchasing it or keeping it. Pianos are subjective and will appeal to each of us in a unique way. This style piano allows an individual to play faster than is physically possible on a smaller piano such as a Spinet or various Consoles. And if the individual playing this piano outgrows it, due to the need for additional finger speed, (s)he would need to upgrade to a horizontal or grand piano. The hammers in a grand piano move up and down as opposed to across to strike the strings.

I had a client with a three year old boy who was very curious and aware of his surroundings. When he was 2 years old, he made his mother put sheet music on the piano whenever he sat down to play because he knew that was what she did when she was playing.

When he was three years old, his mother invited some of his friends to come to their house to play while I was tuning. When they asked him who I was, he said "Oh, she is the piano doctor. She puts batteries in the piano to fix it."

Two weeks later, I was at another home when I heard a buzz coming from the piano. When I opened it up, I found two batteries! The gentleman said his grandchildren thought all pianos were electronic, so they put batteries inside to help. That's when he was convinced that the instrument needed to be tuned and called me.

And it was at this time that I truly realized that a new generation had arrived on the planet.

10

The Grand Style

10. The Grand Style

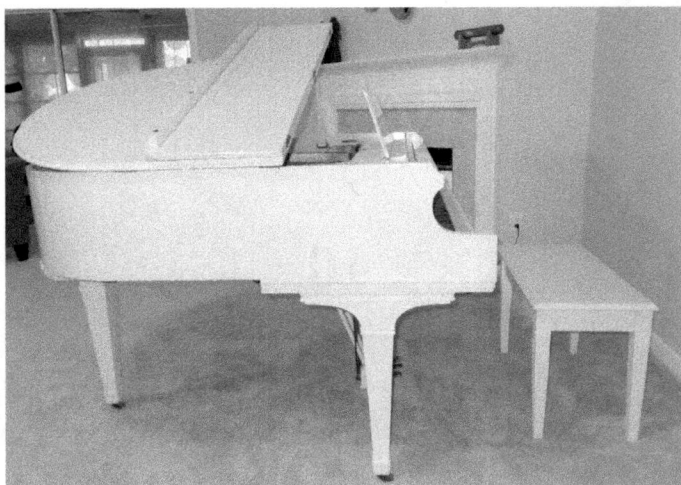

Apartment to Concert Grand
4'7" to over 10' long

There were various styles of grand pianos developed and called
pianofortes or forte pianos.*

The first "PianoForte" is credited in the year 1707 to Bartolomo
Christofori. As the grand piano evolved, there was a demand
for a more sophisticated action and thicker strings that could
produce more volume. The first "Grand Pianoforte" was a
concert piano designed and named by Robert Stodart in 1790.**
In the year 1828 he developed the first grand piano to have
an almost completely metal frame. It solved the problem of
needing increased tension for thicker piano strings which were
used to obtain greater volume. It had 78 light narrow keys. The

* Pianos and their Makers, 1972
** The National Museum of American History

modern grand was completed at the end of the 19th century. It contained an iron frame, greater volume, 88 keys and 3 pedals.* Variations are still being made in pianos today.

Grand pianos are horizontal pianos. They range in length from in front of the keyboard to the back of the piano from four feet seven inches to greater than ten feet. Research identifies general length guidelines as follows:

Apartment Size Grand: 4' 7"

Baby Grand: 5' to 5'4"

Medium Grand: 5'5" to 5'9"

Living Room Grand: 5'10" to 6'1"

Parlor Grand: 6'2" to 6'9"

Music Room/Small Concert Grand: 6'10" to 7' 10"

Full Concert Grand: 9' or longer

There are differences of opinion on how grand pianos are categorized. I noted that my instructor at the New England Conservatory identified all pianos that were 5'10" and smaller as baby grands. Grand pianos were identified as 5'10.5" and longer. Concert grands were identified as nine feet or longer.

For further information on this topic, two good sources are *The Wonders of the Piano*** and *www.steinwaypianos.com.*

* Smithsonian Music 2013
** The Wonders of The Piano, 1992

Smaller halls may host grand pianos that are six or seven feet long for concerts. The size of the room and its unique acoustics may determine the required size of the piano.

Concert grands begin their length at 9 feet. This enables the individual who is sitting in the last row of a concert hall to be able to hear the instrument with the top open. The longer strings can produce clearer and cleaner sounds. Artists will choose which available piano they would like to play, as no two pianos are identical.

Bosendorfer produces two concert grand pianos with additional keys in the bass if desired. One model is extended to 92 notes. The Imperial model has an additional octave.*

Yamaha manufactures grand and upright "silent pianos". While you play the piano, a digital sensor "transmits your performance silently to you through your stereo headphones".**

As developments continue, the largest concert piano to date is the Fazioli concert piano, model F308 which is 10 feet 2 inches long. It is designed and manufactured in Italy. It has four pedals. The fourth pedal is designed to allow the artist to "reduce volume without modifying timbre".***

* *Bosendorfer.com*
** *Yamaha. com*
*** *Fazioli.com*

Expose My Keys

Pull up the fallboard to expose the keys if the cover is closed. The photo to the right will show you how, if you do not already know.

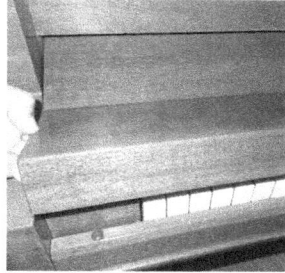

The Fallboard

Remove My Music Desk

Music Desk

Slide the music desk evenly toward you with both hands. The desk holds the music that you read while playing. See the side slots in this style piano.

Certain music desks must be slid forward slightly and lifted out of a slot.

Slot Release Style

Check My Hinges

Move to the left side of the piano to check and make sure that there are hinges with hinge pins in place before the top is raised. If that is not the case, *do not lift the top*. Also make sure there are no cracks around that area. The top could fall off when lifted.

Hinges are important. Make sure that the top is connected on the side before lifting.

Lift My Top

After viewing the hinges, if it is safe to lift the top, raise it with assistance as you support it with its prop stick. Do not let your assistant let the top go until you both verify that the stick does not wobble and is securely placed in the support groove as seen in the following photograph.

Support Groove

Prop Stick

How to Perform a Visual Check

Observe the following photographs. They identify various parts of a grand piano. If you take photo notes of the condition of the parts in the piano that you are observing, these will act as your guide in identifying the attributes of the piano. Photo notes can also point out questions that you need to have answered.

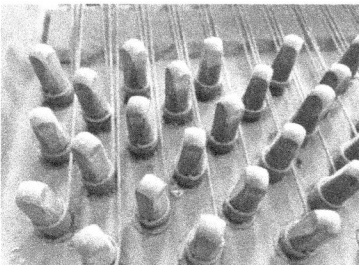

Tuning Pins and Strings

The tuning pins and strings to the left are rusty. They will need to be replaced.

These tuning pins and strings are in good shape. Note the the lack of rust on the fine graded steel tenor and treble wire, and the tuning pins.

Bass Strings are wound strings usually made of copper. When they are new, they are an orange-looking color. As they age, they get darker.

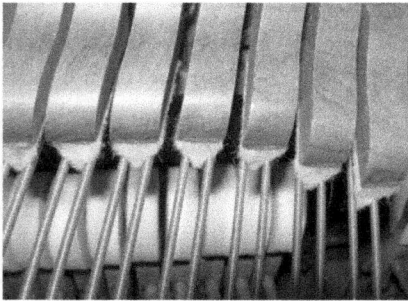

These parts are in good shape.

Dampers on top

Wound Bass Strings
White Hammers below

Iron bass strings can be found in some of the older pianos. As iron is no longer being used, if you see it in a piano, it may be quite old. These wound strings have a slightly dull silver look.

One evening I received a call from an owner who said that her cat walked on the piano keys at night, occasionally waking them up. Sometimes he would jump up and climb inside the baby grand piano.

Well, as the cat grew older, it grew bigger in size. The previous evening it climbed into the piano as usual. When they heard him screaming, they rushed downstairs and found him stuck under the strings. They eased his massive furry body out of the piano.

They called me in the morning to ask if the bass strings were supposed to be green? I told them that I would be right over!

The piano had an indescribable odor. Aye, aye, aye, I thought, and informed the owners that the strings had to be replaced. The piano also had to be disinfected.

And by the way, the strings were supposed to be copper orange!!!

Tenor and Treble Strings are not wound like bass strings. They are steel wires.

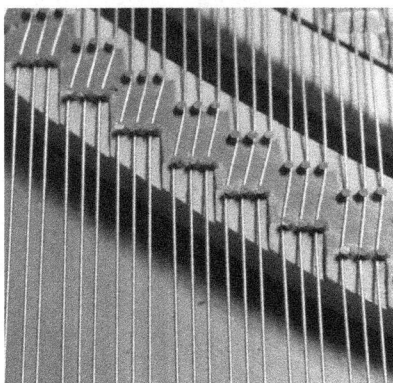

Fine grain steel piano wire for the tenor and treble strings

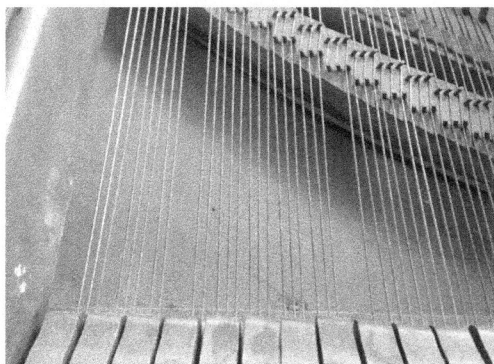

Missing Strings

In this piano there are missing strings. They will need to be replaced. If they are not replaced, when the hammers strike the strings, the hammer heads will wear unevenly.

The Dampers sit on top of the strings to keep them quiet when not in use. Dampers in good condition, like those to the right, are white and not frayed, worn, or stained.

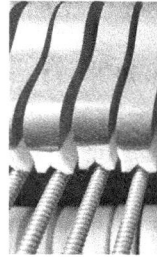

The Hammers reside below the strings. If they are not white, then they are probably old and or brittle. If the tops contain deep grooves then they are probably quite worn. A technician can indicate when they need to be replaced or if they can in fact be refurbished. I have found wine stains and beverage stains on school and household piano hammers. This is not a good find.

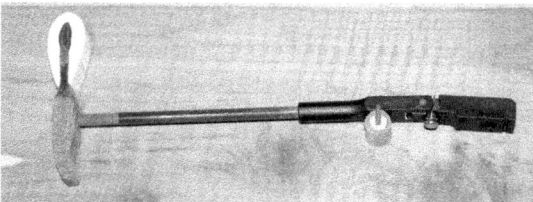

Hammer shanks hold the hammer heads. This photo shows a carbon shank.

Hammer Shanks are usually make of wood but may on occasion be made of another substance. The shanks hold the hammer heads. If you notice black shanks attached to the hammers instead of wood as you are looking through the strings, these are quality made carbon shanks made by Wessell, Nickel & Gross.* They may also be found in newer pianos as they are now becoming more common.

*Appendix

The Wooden Bridges support the strings and the **Bridge Pins** guide the angle of the strings.

If there are cracks in the bridges, this could cause a change in tension on the piano wire. And this could distort the sound. If the bridges are coming unglued at the soundboard, this would be a major repair. Stability would be compromised. When you play, if tiny cracks do not affect the sound, these minor cracks may not be an immediate problem.

The Soundboard resides under the strings. If the soundboard separates from the ribs that give it support on the bottom side, it may cause the piano to buzz. This can be repaired.

Large cracks can be the result of the age of the piano or the instrument being too close to a radiator or wood burning stove. During your initial listening tests, this piano passed. If you are the owner of this instrument you will have to contact a technician to check your piano in the instance that it has a buzz. The ultimate question should be: Do I like the sound of this piano?

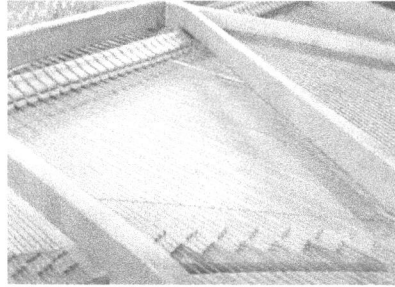

Crack in a soundboard

The Piano Case condition should be noted. Is it in great shape, chipped, scratched or water marked by a vase that had been put on the top for decoration?

The Keytops are important to note as well. Are they chipped, cracked, uneven or missing? They can be replaced. Are they

plastic or ivory? Don't know? Chapter 13 will provide you with the answers.

The ultimate question for you here is: Do I like the feel of the keys?

The Number of Pedals Vary. The most common Grand Pianos have three pedals. There are some Grand Pianos that only have two pedals; and there are some Grand Pianos that were designed for three pedals, but only two pedals function. These pedals are the soft pedal on the left and the damper pedal on the right.

The soft pedal or *una corda pedal* shifts the entire keyboard to the right to soften the sound. For example, when the keyboard shifts, only two of three strings will now be heard, thus softening the sound. The pedal in the middle is called the sostenuto or sustain pedal. It lifts a rail that allows the pianist to hold down a chord and then allows the pianist to play single notes on top of the chord as the chord sustains its tone. However, it may just be attached for show. The pedal on the right lifts the dampers away from the strings so the notes will not be muffled when played. If one pedal is not working, a qualified technician can inspect the mechanism and give you an answer about its functionality.

Please note that the 10' 2" Fazioli grand has four pedals.

The Color of the Wood should be noted when you look inside the grand piano from above as well as the condition of the strings and tuning pins. Dark wood and rusty strings result from too much moisture and age. Cracks indicate dryness.

The Piano Action in a Grand Piano should only be removed by a qualified technician. There are too many variables that could cause a novice to damage the instrument. Therefore, its removal is not being discussed in this book.

Grand Piano Action

My Level of Efficiency

The keys in a grand piano move the hammers up and down with the assistance of gravity. Larger pianos can accommodate longer strings which can produce a cleaner sound. The movement of the key traveling up and down rather than across to reach the strings is more efficient. Unlike a vertical piano, this enables piano players to move their fingers at a faster pace if desired.

Will My Grand Style Benefit You?

Anyone who would enjoy playing an efficiently designed piano action would benefit by this style. As I have pointed out earlier, each piano is different.

You must locate a specific piano that strikes your fancy, your space requirements and your budget.

It was a warm, sunny day in the countryside as I tuned a nine foot long Steinway Grand Piano that could be heard outside the client's floor to ceiling picture window. Suddenly, a yellow shafted flicker appeared. I struck a note on the piano and it flew into the window to get closer to the sound! It was okay. It was hovering again.

This happened five times. I kept checking to make sure that it was still alive! Finally, it flew away. I don't know if anyone else has noticed, but birds appear to be attracted to the sound of the strings. I often see them in the trees and bushes outside a window while I'm tuning. And when I stop, they disappear.

11

Player Pianos

11. Player Pianos

The first player piano mechanism was invented in 1731 by Justinian Morse of England.* They were introduced to the public in the 1890s. And yes, we still find them in homes today.

Old Style Upright Players

These instruments will open like all of the other vertical pianos. If the piano you are viewing has a player system in it, ask to see it play. The piano action will be behind the player mechanism. If it has been maintained, it can bring you many pleasurable hours. If the piano and player mechanism have been neglected and need to be refurbished, it could be quite costly to repair these systems.

I have had to disassemble Upright Player Pianos to allow me to repair the piano action located behind their mechanisms. The owners did not want to invest in a total overhaul of the piano as they were just interested in playing the piano.

One identifying clue that an Upright Piano was a former Player Piano will be control nobs located in front of the keys. Sometimes the controls have a cover in front of them. If you see a panel of wood in front of the keys connected to hinges, pull it down to reveal nobs designed to adjust the Player.

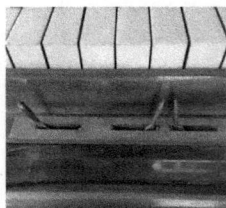

* *Pianos and their Makers (1972), Piano Servicing Tuning & Rebuilding (1993)*

Music Desk Area of an Upright Player Piano

Another clue would be the music desk area. Player panels would open in the front to insert the piano player rolls. If you moved your sheet music aside and opened up the panel behind the music desk, the Player mechanism could be seen. The music rolls were placed on the device behind this panel.

The Bottom Panel was designed to slide open. The Player Pedals were often folded up inside when not in use. Some of these pianos had to be pumped by pushing on the pedals to enable the music rolls to play.

Old Style Grand Players

Grand player instruments did exist as well. So it is possible that you might encounter one that still has a player mechanism. A horizontal or grand piano that has had its mechanism removed can be identified as a former player piano, when some of the case parts are removed by a piano technician.

Holes that have been cut out of the piano to hold a player mechanism will be revealed.

This piano contains keys that are extra long. The holes once held a player mechanism used to push down on the keys. When the keys were pushed down, the hammers would rise to strike the strings.

Modern Player Systems

Modern player pianos have come a long way. They can be used with computers and home entertainment systems. They are acoustic pianos with player mechanisms attached. You will see either a control unit below

the keyboard, on top of the piano, or beside the piano depending on the system and how it is being used. It may also be hidden.

The wiring is concealed. The owners of these pianos should be able to demonstrate to you how they work. Check to make sure that they are operational. Allow the owner to display all of their features, and ask who has been servicing the mechanism.

- The Yamaha Disklavier hybrid acoustic/digital piano was introduced in 1986 with "high performance solenoids and state of the art computer technology".* Its models include a "silent system" that allows one to play the piano silently using headphones.

- Piano Disc is a hybrid first introduced in 1989 that converts a modern piano for use with an MP3, CD, DVD, iPod, iPad and more.*

- QRS Player Pianos play CDs, DVDs, MP3s, can access the QRS radio function and play music from piano player roles purchased from their catalog.*

Appendix

I have been servicing a piano at a home for many years with a small gray and black terrier with a spattering of white undertones. When he sits on his hind legs and attentively looks up at the piano, he looks like he should be wearing a bow tie.

When I strike a certain range of notes in the tenor section of the piano, he begins to grunt. Slowly, he matches my rhythm and begins to sing. He matches each note perfectly, in a howl-like manner. I have to break up the rhythm to get him to stop so I can hear the notes I am playing. I hate to do it, but his singing is really loud.

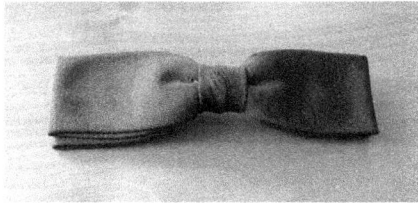

12

Bird Cage Pianos

12. Bird Cage Pianos

I place pianos with Bird Cage Actions in the family of unusual pianos.

Bird Cage Actions are European pianos that are not commonly found in the United States. The action contains wires that look like a bird cage. These wires make it difficult to tune evenly as they are a barrier to reaching the strings.

Do not be fooled by beautiful cases with complex actions. You may be asking for trouble. Trying to get a clean sound out of them may be quite problematic.

13

Are My Keys
Ivory or Plastic?

13. Are My Keys Ivory or Plastic?

Ivory keytops usually consist of two pieces. The majority of ivory pieces for piano keytops consist of a head and a tail as indicated by a split or fine line in the ivories.

Tails

Heads

Ivory, which is bone, is porous. Pianists who would sweat a great deal while playing were able to grip ivory since it was porous and prevented their fingers from sliding off the keys.*

Elephant ivory bone is thin. In order to prevent one from seeing through it to the color of the wood that it rests upon, there is a layer of cheese cloth under the ivory to help give the key its light color.

Ivory tends to yellow when it is kept out of direct sunlight. It is also susceptible to chipping and cracking. CITE, the Convention on International Trade in Endangered Species, monitors the ban on ivory. There was a global ban placed on ivory in 1989. The precise date when all manufacturers stopped using ivory in pianos prior to 1989 is not known.*

* *Elephant Under Glass, 1993*

For updated information one can seek information from the U.S. Fish & Wildlife Service website regarding International Affairs with endangered species. Cracked ivory can be removed and replaced with plastic keytops.

The tops of the keys in front before the line split are called the heads. The white extensions next to the ebony sharp keys are called the tails. As you can note, the thin ivory keys are beginning to split or crack.

Oil and dirt from our fingers naturally make their way into the pores of the ivory. The pores allow just enough friction for the fingers to depress, release and grip the keys. Since they absorb sweat, they need to be cleaned frequently with use.

Plastic keytops are generally one piece. They can vary in color and texture. Plastic was introduced to pianos after World War II .*

Plastic making improved over time. Since 1992, manufacturers have been able to produce ivory-looking plastic for individuals who want the ivory-like look and feel.**

* Appendix
** The Wonders of the Piano, 1992

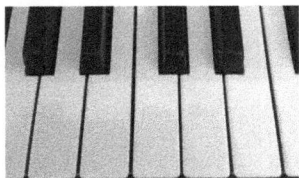

*Modern one-piece plastic key
tops with plastic sharps*

Early Plastic

The owners of a house that I was scheduled to visit left their door open for me to come in and tune at my appointed time. They asked me if I was okay with dogs, and I said yes. When I opened up the door of the modernized rustic farmhouse, a brown and white boxer came out of its crate to greet me with its short wagging tail. I set myself up and began to tune the baby grand piano. All of a sudden, the dog decided to play the piano with me. He took his chin and started banging on the notes. The dog's height was in fact, the general key height for grand pianos. He did not care if the keys were ivory or plastic! And don't be surprised if your animals also play when you're away.

14

How Old Am I?

14. How Old Am I?

You want to know my age? Pianos contain serial numbers that can be researched along with the name of the piano to provide you with this answer. If it is not listed in a piano atlas, by a current manufacturer, original paperwork or on-line, it will remain a secret.

The serial number in vertical and horizontal pianos is usually located inside the piano. It will be marked on the cast iron plate or in a cut-out on the cast iron plate, or even on the original soundboard. It may also be located in upright pianos on the top left side of the casework or underneath in grand pianos.

The serial number along with the brand of piano will allow the piano tuner-technician to look up the age of the piano in a piano atlas.*

When a piano states "established in the year" on the cast iron plate, this indicates when the company was established, not the year the piano was made. This complex instrument may list an established date, a patent date, and part dates on various parts of the piano. Its manufacturer most probably built thousands of pianos.

* *Pierce Piano Atlas*

> **Established**
>
> **1849**
>
> **199410**

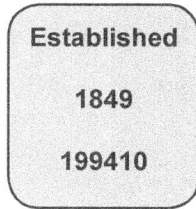

199410 is the "Serial Number"

The serial number is a piano sequencing number that leads to the year a piano maker made a particular series of pianos. The number will not have a space or gap in the sequence. It may, however, have a period between digits as in the example below:

Schimmel Serial Number on Piano 335.00
www.schimmel-pianos.de lists: Year 2005

A piano technician, with a serial number in hand, will go to a piano atlas to look up the year the piano was made by searching a manufacturer's list of numbers and dates.

When I go to a piano atlas to look up the year the piano was built, this is what I see for example. This indicates that the piano was built in 2004.

Yamaha Serial Number on Piano 60660001

Piano Atlas lists: Serial Numbers 6066000-6610999 (Date) 2004

In the following example, the serial number falls within a range which indicates that this piano was built between 1990 and 1995.

Petrof Serial Number on Piano 525882

Piano Atlas lists: Serial Numbers 504500 (Date) 1990

529900 (Date) 1995

Pianos made in countries such as Indonesia and Korea, may have letters instead of numbers to indicate the year like HH, IS or JJ. Identification numbers are still evolving.

The following photo examples should provide you with some clarity in your search for: "How Old Am I?"

Finding My Upright Serial Number

This particular piano listed the serial number in a cutout on the cast iron plate near the tuning pins as well as on the bottom of the soundboard. The cutout is a common area for serial numbers.

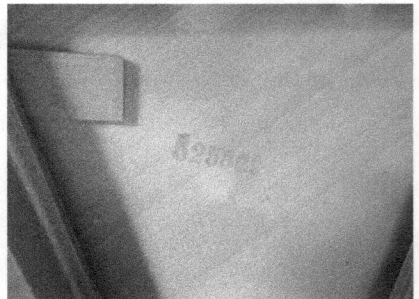

Identifying My Grand ID Number

As you can see in the photos above, there are no breaks in the serial number assigned to these pianos.

The following number is listed on a Sohmer Grand piano.

47311 #9B

Scale A

The number 47311 is the serial number.

The Consequence of No Identification

There are some instances when there are no longer any numbers on a given piano. This may happen when it is refurbished. There are also some instances when the name of the piano cannot be found. Without both the piano brand name and serial number, the age of the piano cannot be determined.

If the piano maker did not manufacture many pianos, the data was lost, or the record keeping system was not maintained, the Piano Atlas may not have any dates for these instruments.

15

Piano Life Saver Systems

15. Piano Life Saver Systems

A Piano Life Saver System* has been designed to create a microclimate for a piano to help maintain a consistent relative humidity level throughout the year. Pianos go out of tune seasonally, when they are moved, played hard consistently, and with fluctuating or extreme environmental changes. Even when a piano is not being played, the wood holding the tuning pins expands and contracts with the environment. The soundboard can crack from a lack of humidity. Piano parts can develop mold and rust from too much humidity.

The optimal piano temperature and humidity are approximately 70 degrees Fahrenheit or 21.1 Celsius along with 45% relative humidity. Want to know how your house is measuring up to these standards? A thermometer and hygrometer will let you know how consistent or inconsistent your temperature and humidity levels become throughout the year.

A complete life system includes a humidifier, dehumidifiers, a water sensor, humidistat, and a three-light panel to aid in maintaining the system's consistency.

* *Appendix*

Flashing lights indicate a need for water or new humidifier pads

In an upright piano the system will be mounted inside the case or behind the piano if there is not enough room inside.

In a grand piano the system will be mounted on the underside of the piano. All units are hidden as much as possible by a certified installer. Please refer to the Appendix to find out how to contact a field expert.

In your travels, you may see a system with a single orange light. This is an older system. New systems have a three-light panel as seen in the photo above. If you come across a silver rod, this is an older dehumidifier that is no longer available. Newer dehumidifiers are black in color.

All new systems are guaranteed for five years. It is recommended that humidifier pads be changed every six months and the system be checked by a technician at least once per year.

The system should remain plugged in at all times to aid in creating a consistent microclimate for the piano that will assist in maintaining the piano's stability.

I had a client who is a performing and recording artist. When she informed me that she was moving to Hawaii, the question she asked me was should she move her Steinway Grand piano to the islands? It rains 6 plus inches a day. Would she be better off getting a lower quality inexpensive piano?

I recommended that she take the Steinway and enjoy her Baby. Any piano that she had in her new home would endure the same environmental challenges. Wouldn't it be better to take a piano that was solidly built and reliable?

I then contacted a qualified technician in Hawaii to obtain information on care for the instrument. My client and I discussed this new information which included installing Piano Life Saver dehumidifiers underneath her piano.

She now has a new qualified tuner-technician contact in her new location. Because he has a good reputation, she can trust his recommendations for keeping her piano in excellent condition.

16

Why Contact a Qualified Technician?

16. Why Contact a Qualified Technician?

A qualified piano tuner-technician has a reputation to uphold. The Mission Statement of the Piano Technician's Guild includes *"...to promote the highest possible standards of piano service by providing members with opportunities for professional development by recognizing technical competence through examinations...".* The highest level that can be achieved in the Guild is that of RPT or Registered Piano Technician.*

There are qualified tuners who may no longer be a member of the Guild. How would you know that they are qualified? They could still have a card from the Guild that verifies that they had passed their rigorous examinations. The piano tuner could also be tuning for professional performing artists, in clubs or concert venues.

There are also qualified rebuilders who are not piano tuners, and who are not RPTs. They should have a workshop where you can view their specialty piano work - or better still, get a referral for a rebuilder from a qualified technician.

I Am Old

Looks can be deceiving. The piano in the next photo looks good because the soundboard is in very good condition. As the technician, I discover that the tuning pins, however, are loose and the bass section does not want to stay in tune. One clue is the rust

* Appendix

on some of the strings. This indicates that the piano was in a wet environment.

The tuning pins in the cast iron plate hold the strings.

When the piano action is removed, I am able to look up at the bottom of the tuning pins from inside the piano. A large hidden crack is revealed in the pin block. It can only be felt by hand and by inserting a mirror under the tuning pins, or by sticking my head inside and looking up.

The Wood Pin Block under the plate to the left, holds the tuning pins

When the loose tuning pins that are currently in the pin block are measured, it is revealed that they have been replaced several times and are at their maximum size. Replacing the pin block is not an inexpensive repair. Cost to refurbish this piano is $5700.

Another Example of Hidden Damage

This sharp key looks fine when you look down at it, but what you cannot see is the damage to the key when it is removed

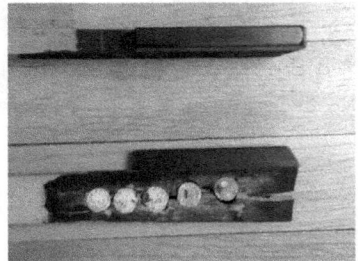

I Do Not Sound Right

When was the last time the piano was tuned? Pianos go out of tune seasonally. Even when they are climatically controlled, they still require tuning. A tuner-technician can let you know if the tuning pins are strong enough to enable a standard tuning.

The hammers may be worn from playing and need to be voiced* to provide an even sound. It is possible that they may need to be replaced. Other worn parts that affect the sound include worn out dampers and old strings.

My Touch Does Not Feel Right

When was the last time the piano was adjusted? It needs to be tuned up like a car to assure that all parts are functioning properly. Screws come loose. Joints come unglued. Felts get worn out. These parts work together when being played and if one part is worn, loose or broken, it will affect another part. A technician will provide you with the estimates you will need for adjustments or repairs.

I Am a Buy Me Piano

A qualified technician can let you know if the piano is structurally sound. S(he) can let you know if the piano can be tuned to standard pitch. The technician can also provide you with estimates for multiple tunings if the piano was neglected.

*Under the Lid, 2008

Pianos generally need to be refurbished after 50 years with some exceptions of course. Some pianos may need to have parts replaced sooner and some later. It depends on how well the instrument was maintained. The technician can provide you with the benefits of buying a particular piano that interests you.

Rodent Damage Repairs

If you push down on one or more keys and they don't play, it could be a sign of mice damage. Mice or other small rodents can do significant damage to a piano. In the right environment, they may build nests by using the carpeting from your floors. They may also use asbestos from your walls or batting from pillows and stuff it in the piano next to or under the piano keys. Seeds and nuts are two of their favorite foods. But if you have left out food, pet food or candy, they will have snacks while running in and out of the piano.

If you see some semblance of a nest on the left or right hand side of the keys and the keys are sticky, this piano will require a technician to give you a price on rectifying any damage. It could be a matter of just cleaning out the piano or repairing extensive damage.

In extreme situations, rodents will chew piano felt and wood as well as corrode piano wire. I would recommend leaving this job to the technician who will advise you about rodent control.

The photo above reveals a nest hidden under the piano case in an upright piano.

The photos below show the damage these same mice did with chewing the key felts and chewing the wood of the keys as well.

chewed felt

chewed keys

127

A client, who was also a friend, called me and said there was a problem with her piano. I had tuned it 3 months earlier. She was going to give the piano to a school as a gift. But just before the move was going to take place, the piano keys began to stick.

As soon as I opened up the piano, I noticed a mouse nest in the left corner by the keys. So, I began to clean it out while three of her cats nonchalantly watched me.

After I cleaned out the corner I noticed a few notes sticking in the middle of the piano. When I lifted up the keys, I saw a bracelet-like object. I mentioned to the owner that it had not been there 3 months before.

When I pulled out my long tweezers to pull it out, it moved. It was the tail of a mouse hiding from me. The mouse began to run back and forth under the piano keys, while the cats watched with disinterest. I tried to catch it with a jar and with everything else that was within my reach without success.

Then the mouse chewed its way through straps towards the bottom of the piano and escaped. It kept peeking out at me from behind the piano. The owner didn't have the heart to catch it and the cats were not interested. And now I had to repair the damage with new parts before the piano was given away and trust that she moved the piano the day after my repairs!

My friend gave me a catnip mouse on my birthday as a reminder of my unusual experience as a piano tuner-technician in her home music studio.

I received a call from a client with a grand piano.

"I dropped a pencil in the piano right after you left. Can you return?"

"I can come tomorrow," I replied.

He said, "Never mind. I know how to open up the piano and pull out the action."

"No, please wait for me to come!"

He assured me that he had watched how it was pulled out and that it would not be a problem.

"Okay, let me know if I can be of any further assistance," I said.

No more than fifteen minutes later, Tom called me back to let me know that he had broken off the tops of several hammers while attempting to remove the action and was ready to make another appointment.

Estimates for Maintenance, Repair, Reconditioning

Each time the piano is tuned, it should be checked for loose screws and any other required adjustments. After your piano is tuned, it is less expensive to let a qualified technician set a date for adjustments or repair than it is to wait for a part to break or wear out.

If a piano is more than 100 years old, it would be prudent to make sure that replacement parts are still available. This is also true for Spinet Pianos that are no longer being manufactured.

The Chaplain at an Air Force Base had to have the grand piano tuned on this particular day in the Chapel. As I began to tune, roofers began to take apart the roof. The pounding was fierce.

It caused ceiling debris to fall into the top of the now open grand piano. I could barely hear.

The Chaplain may have been partially deaf from being around airplanes. He did not notice the noise. And when I finished, he said, "The piano sounds so good!"

Knowing what you like to hear is subjective.

17

Care For Your Piano

17. Care for Your Piano:

Piano care is for those who want their investment to be in the best possible condition. This instrument is a work of art. It is designed to provide you with a lifetime of enjoyment when maintained appropriately. In return, the piano can provide one with many hours of enjoyment. For some, it is a stress reliever.

How Do You Contact a Qualified Technician?

A Registered Piano Technician, who is also referred to as an RPT, is a member of The Piano Technicians Guild. All RPTs had to pass rigorous tuning and technical exams to qualify for their title. It is their job to provide you with expert service worthy of any piano.

Registered Technicians can be located by going to the Piano Technicians Guild website, www.PTG.org. On this site you will have access to a data base of qualified technicians. A search by zip code will lead you to the closest technicians in your area.

I Need Routine Tunings

I would recommend that you check with an RPT who lives in your area and has been to your home, school, church, theater or other establishment to find out how many times she or he recommends that your instrument be tuned each year. Factors that affect a piano going out of tune include where it is located in a building, fluctuations with heat and humidity, seasonal changes and how often it is played.

The piano needs to have all items taken off of the piano for tuning and the room needs to be quiet so the tuner can hear and compare the strings that are being tuned to produce a clean sound.

Pianos Need to be Adjusted

Pianos need to be checked for any adjustments that need to be made each time the piano is tuned. This process is called Regulation. Screws need to be tightened, loose parts need to be repaired, hammers need to be voiced to bring out an even tone for example. The piano contains thousands of parts. No need to have loose hammers clicking while playing, or keytops sliding from side to side. Hire an expert and listen to what your qualified technician recommends to allow your piano to function at its best.

When Do You Adjust and Tune Me for Your Concert?

Schedule tunings as close as possible to a concert or performance venue. Concert preparation should be scheduled before the final tuning to assure that all parts of the piano are adjusted appropriately and suit the Artist who will be performing. This includes assuring that the hammer tone is consistent and the piano has an even and responsive touch.*

A same day final tuning is ideal. This is the norm. When the piano is tuned, the temperature of the room and the lighting should be set the same way it will be for the concert to allow for piano stability. As there are more than 200 strings in a piano that are being struck by percussive blows as it is being played, do not be surprised if you see a piano tuner touching up a piano on stage during an intermission. Guitar players sometimes tune their instruments in-between songs. A performing artist as well as the audience appreciates a piano that produces a clean sound that enhances the performance.

Have I Been Placed in the Right Location?

A stable environment with no excessive temperature and humidity changes will help to bring out the colors of the instrument that make up its unique sound.

If possible, do not locate a piano on top of a heating vent or have a vent blowing into the back of an upright piano. These situations will dry out the wood, cause tuning instability and possibly crack various parts of the instrument. This also holds true for a wood burning stove. In this case, the room will require humidity to

*Pianos and their Makers (1972), Under the Lid (2008), My Life with the Great Pianists (1992)

balance out the heat that is being generated. Forty to fifty percent humidity is the goal.

If the instrument is located near an outside door that is being frequently used, be prepared to need more frequent tunings. Wet basements, ocean and wetland locations may pose a problem with rust. A technician can also point out problems such as mold coming from a wet environment and give you advice on potential solutions for these challenges.

Dry and desert-like locations may require humidity.

A hygrometer measures moisture. This device will let you know if your piano location is experiencing wide fluctuations in humidity. It takes the "guess work" out of whether or not the room is stable throughout the year. A technician can purchase one for you.

Pianos that are located in rooms such as churches, where the heat is turned up when the congregation is present and then turned down to a minimum setting when they leave, upset the stability of the piano. These pianos will need to be tuned more often.

Avoid direct sunlight on a piano. It may cause the color to fade. If the sun is strong, its heat could affect the stability of the piano.

Clean My Keytops

Keytops can be cleaned with a little dish washing liquid, water, paper towels or soft clean cloths that are preferably white. Colored cloths could possibly stain your keytops; especially if they are made of ivory. Ivory is porous and the color could get into the ridges of the the bone.

Slightly dampen a clean white cloth and add a little dishwashing liquid. Lift up the natural white keys and make sure that no water gets in-between the keys. Immediately wipe off the liquid with a paper towel or clean cloth.

Repeat the procedure for each plastic sharp. If you look closely at plastic sharps that have been soiled, the surface will not look smooth. The spotting you see will be smudges.

Wooden ebony sharps are stained and you do not want the stain to rub onto the natural white keys. Use clean cloths.

If you prefer to use a ready mix solution to clean your keytops, there is a product manufactured for ivory and plastic to clean the keys. Ask your technician for a bottle of Cory Key Brite.

Please do not use a non-sanctioned product like hand sanitizer or any other solvents as there is a possibility that they may stain your keys permanently.

Case Cleaning

If the piano is new, check the owner's manual.

Dust? Use a feather duster. This will also prevent you from scratching a piano that has a lacquer or high gloss finish.

Moisture? Avoid putting plants on a piano. The pots may leave an indentation in the finish and when they are watered, the moisture may damage the case. Leaving a drink on the piano case may have the same affect.

Fingerprints? Smudges? Use a slightly damp clean cloth made of a flannel-like material or felt. A technician can provide you with a cloth designed to clean the case if one did not come with the piano.

If you need a little more oomph, add a little Murphy's Oil Soap to the damp cloth.

Polishing? Avoid sprays, silicone, and inexpensive furniture polish. The safest way to protect the finish is to obtain a bottle of piano polish from a qualified technician. These polishes have been designed specifically for your piano.

A technician is the only qualified individual to work on the inside of a piano and prevent any damage from being done to delicate areas. Please do not attempt to clean the inside.

Measuring Humidity

Not sure if your piano is located in an environment with extreme changes in humidity? Purchase a hygrometer. The ideal humidity is between 40 and 50%. On the east coast we struggle to get the humidity down from 60% or higher in the summer, and struggle to get it above 35% in the winter, unless the piano is located on the ocean.

Are You Moving Me?

Pianos that are moved should be tuned after being moved. In the event that the piano is moving from one home to another, wait several weeks to allow the piano to acclimate to its new location. Make sure that you hire qualified piano movers. They should also be insured.

There was a senior piano tuner-technician in our PTG Chapter whose name was Dick. The Piano Chapter members would meet at his home workshop to work on piano projects. One day a technician asked someone to pass the thing-a-ma-jig. As it was being passed, Dick blurted out "None of you technicians know piano nomenclature!"

Suddenly one technician said, "Sure we do. That's the doo-higgy that allows the thing-a-ma-jig to work." We doubled over with laughter by the sour look on his face.

As you can see, technicians know how to communicate with each other?!!

Dick just shook his head.

Tuning a piano for a cancer hospital has its rewards. In the lobby is a recently donated baby grand with a player mechanism attached. It plays softly to calm the thoughts and feelings of those who pass through or wait patiently for news about those whom they love.

Each time I arrive I am greeted by either a long term patient, doctor or visitor. They always approach my right side with a smile and ask a question that has been on their mind about pianos or tell me stories about their own experiences. They are from all walks of life. Why they are in the hospital is their commonality. Each of their thanks to me is precious.

18

Save Time & Money

18. Save Time & Money

Save money with regular piano maintenance. Ask how your piano is doing. **Yes, Piano, How Are You!** It's an exciting purchase.

By hiring a qualified piano tuner-technician, you can be assured that your investment is receiving the best of care. You will not be hiring someone twice to do a task that should have been resolved the first time. If the technician is perplexed by a problem, other Piano Technician Guild members are always willing to assist by sharing their past experiences and expertise.

If you are considering buying a piano, you are now equipped to do certain tests to determine if you want to hire an RPT to test the instrument technically. You do not have to hire someone to accompany you to look at each piano beforehand. You have a knowledge of piano styles, basic questions to ask a technician, and questions to ask and answer yourself, before you spend money hiring anyone.

As you view and assess pianos you should find that you have an increased understanding about these instruments. You will know that a piano needs to be maintained as well as tuned, and when and how to contact a qualified technician in your area.

This new knowledge can be fun, save you money, time and give you additional confidence.

Keep informed.

Never hesitate to ask a question.

Protect your investment.

May you find a gem of a piano!

Universal Appeal

19

Appendix

19. Appendix

Ivory: Connecticuthistory.org/ivory-cutting-the-rise-and-decline-of-a-connecticut-industry/

Pianoasart.com

Find updates from the US Fish and Wildlife Service at *www.fws.gov/international/wildlife-trafficking/index.html.*

Player Pianos:

- View Yamaha Disklavier at the Yamaha.com website
- View Piano Disc Systems information at Pianodiscplayer.com
- View QRS Player Piano Systems at QRSmusic.com

Piano Life Saver Systems: Information can be found at Pianolifesaver.com. The site can provide you with a list of qualified installers in your area. You can then choose your specific country and state to locate a certified installer in your area.

Piano Technicians Guild: This is an organization of craftspeople in the field of piano technology. It was formed to promote the highest possible industry standards, recognize individuals who have achieved technical competence through rigorous exams and certify their achivements with the title of Registered Piano Technician or RPT.

Qualified Piano Tuner Technicians: RPT's or Registered Piano Technicians are members of The Piano Technicians Guild. Go to www.PTG.org and search by zip code to locate qualified Tuner-Technicians in your area.

Wessell, Nickel & Gross: WNG High Performance Piano Parts. Founded in 1874. www.wessellnickelandgross.com

20

Index

Photo Credits:

© Istockphoto p. 30,46, 140,144,156

Nancy Depew, p. 70

Elizabeth Van der Ham, p. 110

Courtesy: Piano Life Saver Systems, p. 119

Anthony Rugnetta, back cover

21

Bibliography

Bibliography

Bielefeldt, Catherine C.   *The Wonders of The Piano*, The Anatomy
of The Instrument, Illinois, 1992

Brady, Stephen   *Under The Lid*, The Art & Craft of the
Concert Piano Technician, Washington,
2008

Dolge, Alfred   *PIANOS and their MAKERS*
New York, 1972

Mohr, Franz   *My Life with the Great Pianists*
Michigan, 1992

Pierce, Bob   *Pierce Piano Atlas*
12th Edition, New Mexico, 2008

Reblitz, Arthur A.

Piano Servicing Tuning & Rebuilding

For The Professional The Student The Hobbyist

Second Edition, New York, 1993

Shayt, David H.

Elephant Under Glass: The Piano Key Bleach

House of Deep River, Connecticut

The Journal of the Society for Industrial

Archeology, Volume 19, No. 1, 1993 and

Reprinted in the Piano Technicians

Journal, July 1995

Smithsonian Music

The Definitive Visual History

DK Publishing 2013

White, William Braid

Piano Tuning And Allied Arts

5th Edition, Boston, 1946

22

About the Author

22. About the Author

Keena Keel formally studied and was certified in her craft at the New England Conservatory of Music's Piano Technology Program. As a former recording artist who loved the sound of the instrument that accompanied her while she sang, she felt that this was a profession that she would enjoy. Ultimately Keena earned the highest title of Registered Piano Tuner Technician through the Piano Technicians Guild and earned the title of Field Expert with Piano Life Saver Systems.

Keena tunes by ear. Her expertise encompasses orchestras, recording studios, jazz festivals, chamber music, performing/recording artists, theaters, music schools, teachers and everyday piano players from her surrounding community. She has also served as a college and university technician.

This book has been developed to answer the everyday questions that she is asked in the field by her clients out of curiosity and by those who are buying and selling their pianos. She is aware that the knowledge that she provides will bring additional clarity, understanding and some inside humor from the piano technician's world.

Keena hopes that you will value and protect your instrument. In return, it should bring you many years of enjoyment.

www.ingramcontent.com/pod-product-compliance
Lightning Source LLC
Chambersburg PA
CBHW072136020426
42334CB00018B/1823